Amazing Animals
Butterflies

Please visit our web site at www.garethstevens.com
For a free catalog describing our list of high-quality books, call 1-800-542-2595 (USA) or 1-800-387-3178 (Canada).
Our fax: 1-877-542-2596

Library of Congress Cataloging-in-Publication Data

Barnard, Edward S.
    Butterflies / by Edward S. Barnard.
        p. cm.—(Amazing Animals)
        Originally published: Pleasantville, NY: Reader's Digest Young Families, c2006.
        Includes bibliographical references and index.
        ISBN-10: 0-8368-9094-9   ISBN-13: 978-0-8368-9094-5 (lib. bdg.)
    1. Butterflies—Juvenile literature. I. Title.
    QL544.2.B378 2009
    595.78'9—dc22   2008013363

This edition first published in 2009 by
Gareth Stevens Publishing
A Weekly Reader® Company
1 Reader's Digest Road
Pleasantville, NY 10570-7000 USA

This edition copyright © 2009 by Gareth Stevens, Inc. Original edition copyright © 2006 by Reader's Digest Young Families, Pleasantville, NY 10570

Gareth Stevens Senior Managing Editor: Lisa M. Herrington
Gareth Stevens Creative Director: Lisa Donovan
Gareth Stevens Art Director: Ken Crossland
Gareth Stevens Associate Editor: Amanda Hudson

Consultant: Robert E. Budliger (Retired), NY State Department of Environmental Conservation

Photo Credits
Cover: Corel Corporation, Title page iStockphoto.com/narcisa-floricica buzlea, Contents page: Dreamstime.com/Jack Schiffer, pages 6-7: iStockphoto.com/Eliza Snow, 8: iStockphoto.com/Ron Brancato, 9 composite: (egg) Eduard Zubli; (caterpiller) iStockphoto.com/Terry J. Alcorn, 10: iStockphoto.com/Ellen Poche, 11 (large): iStockphoto.com/Toya, 11 (inset): iStockphoto.com/Bonnie Schupp, 12: Nova Development Corporation, 13: Corel Corporation, 14-15: Dreamstime.com/Bill Kennedy, 16: Corel Corporation, 17 (illustration): Dreamstime.com/Gennadi Kurilin, 18: (left) Dreamstime.com/David Geneve; (right) iStockphoto.com/Daniel Hyams, 19: iStockphoto.com/James E. Hernandez, 20-21: iStockphoto.com/Sascha Burkard, 21: Dreamstime.com/Olga Mirenska, 22: iStockphoto.com/Janeen Wassink, 23: Corel Corporation, 24-25: Nova Development Corporation, 26: iStockphoto.com/MediaMoments, 27: iStockphoto.com/Scott Hellmann, 28: PhotoDisc/Getty Images, 29: iStockphoto.com/Diane Diederich, 30-31: Dreamstime.com/Vladimir Gurov, 32: iStockphoto.com/Alexander Omelko, 33: Dreamstime.com/Gumenuk Vitalij, 34: Corel Corporation, 35 (large): iStockphoto.com/Viktor Kitaykin, 35 (inset): Corel Corporation, 36-37: iStockphoto.com/Tan Kian Khoon, 38: Dreamstime/Anette linnea Rasmussen, 39: Erin Silversmith, 40: iStockphoto.com/Ryan Poling, 41: iStockphoto.com/Kate Leigh, 43: Dreamstime.com/Valeriy Kalyuzhnyy, 44-45: iStockphoto.com/hd connelly photography, 46: Corel Corporation, Back cover: iStockphoto.com/Scott Hellmann.

Printed in the United States of America

1 2 3 4 5 6 7 8 9 10 09 08

Amazing Animals
Butterflies

By Edward S. Barnard

Gareth Stevens
Publishing

A WEEKLY READER COMPANY

Contents

Chapter 1

A Butterfly Grows Up

No Place Like Home

Female monarch butterflies lay their tiny eggs on milkweed plants. They choose a plant they like by tasting and smelling it with sensors in their feet.

In late summer a female monarch butterfly flits across a meadow. She is carrying more than 300 eggs inside her body. Soon she lays her eggs on milkweed plants. She puts one tiny, sticky egg underneath each leaf.

The egg cracks open in two weeks. A tiny **caterpillar** crawls out. The caterpillar eats her eggshell and nibbles on a leaf. During her first day of life, the caterpillar eats so much that her weight doubles! Every two or three days, she grows so big that the skin covering her body splits open. Then a plumper caterpillar crawls out. Finally, after shedding her fourth skin, the caterpillar is nearly two inches (51 centimeters) long. She is more than 3,000 times heavier than at her birth!

Milkweed Meals

A monarch caterpillar that has hatched from an egg eats only milkweed leaves.

When the caterpillar is finished eating, she leaves the milkweed plant. She weaves a sticky button of silk underneath a new leaf. The caterpillar glues herself onto it, head down. As she dangles, she sheds her skin one last time. Now she is covered by a green case called a **chrysalis**.

In about ten days, orange-and-black wings are visible through the now see-through walls of the case. Finally the walls crack open, and a damp, crumpled female monarch butterfly crawls out.

For a few hours the butterfly clings to the case, resting. Fluids from her body flow into her wing veins. As the veins dry and harden, her wings become rigid. Then she is able to fly away over the meadow.

Time to Transform

After two weeks of eating milkweed leaves, a monarch caterpillar glues the end of its body to the underside of a leaf. Then it wriggles until its skin splits to reveal the chrysalis.

chrysalis

When a monarch butterfly comes out of its chrysalis, its wings are wet and wrinkled.

Wild Words

A **chrysalis** (KRISS a liss) is the case that covers and protects a butterfly's pupa. A **pupa** is a resting stage when a butterfly caterpillar changes to an adult butterfly.

Once in a Lifetime

Millions of monarch butterflies fly south every fall from the northern United States. They fly back north in the spring. Butterflies **migrate** only once. Their children or grandchildren make the trip the following year.

As many as 250 million monarch butterflies spend the winter in Mexico every year. Thousands of monarchs perch on a single fir tree!

It is autumn now, and daytime is getting shorter. The butterfly heads south. She stops to sip **nectar** from flowers. On windy afternoons she soars high up in the air, moving as fast as 70 miles (113 kilometers) an hour.

When she reaches the Sierra Madre highlands of Mexico, she settles on a fir tree. Thousands of other monarchs rest around her. She stays in a state of semi-hibernation for the winter. In March when the sun warms her, she and thousands of other monarchs fly north. After mating with a male monarch, she flies to Texas. Soon after she lays her eggs on milkweed plants, she dies. But the next monarch generation will continue flying north. And later generations will fly back to Mexico.

Bad Taste Here!

Monarch caterpillars are not affected by poison in the milkweed plants they eat. Monarch butterflies carry the poison and taste so bad that predators usually leave them alone.

Chapter 2
A Butterfly's Body

A butterfly has four wings — two forewings and two hindwings. The wing markings are different for each kind of butterfly.

Three in One

Butterflies are insects. Like all insects, their bodies are divided into three parts—the head, **thorax**, and **abdomen**.

Many of a butterfly's sense organs are located in its head, including its eyes, two **antennas** for touching and smelling, and a mouthpart for drinking. The mouthpart is a long tube called a **proboscis** (pronounced pro BOS iss). Inside the head is the butterfly's brain.

The thorax is the anchor point for the butterfly's two pairs of wings and its three pairs of legs. The legs have tasting and smelling sensors on their ends! Inside the thorax are muscles for the wings and legs and for the butterfly's heart.

Behind a butterfly's thorax is the abdomen. It contains a series of tubes that circulates air throughout the body. It also contains organs for reproduction and digestion.

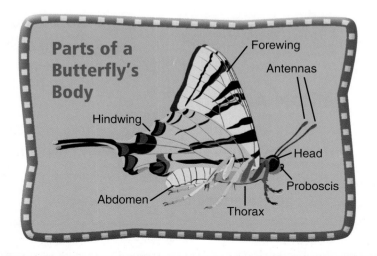

Parts of a Butterfly's Body

Forewing

Antennas

Hindwing

Head

Proboscis

Abdomen

Thorax

Butterfly or Moth?

Butterflies and moths are the only insects with scales on their wings. Scales are what give the wings their color. Butterflies and moths look a lot alike, but there are differences that will help you tell them apart.

- Butterfly antennas have little knobs on their ends or their ends are thicker. Moth antennas never have knobs.

- Butterflies have thinner bodies than moths.

- Most butterflies fly during the day. Most moths fly at night.

- Butterflies often rest with their wings held straight up. Moths usually spread their wings flat.

- Butterflies have less body hair than moths.

Moth

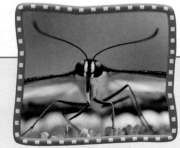

Butterfly

Telltale Antennas

Butterflies and moths use their antennas to smell, which helps them find food and mates. Moths are active at night, when it is harder to see. Their antennas are often larger and more sensitive.

The cecropia moth is the largest moth in North America. It has a wingspan of 5 to 6 inches (13 to 15 cm). Cecropias live just long enough to mate. They never eat!

A Puddle Crowd

Some kinds of butterflies, such as swallowtails and blues, gather in groups as they drink from puddles.

When a butterfly isn't feeding, it keeps its proboscis coiled like a garden hose.

proboscis

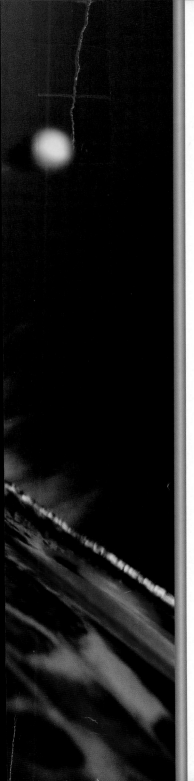

Straw Sipper

Unlike a caterpillar, a butterfly can't chew. It can only sip liquids. It uses its mouthpart (the proboscis) like a straw, poking into flowers and sucking up their sugary nectar. The proboscis can be longer than the butterfly's body!

Eye Contact

A butterfly's eyes are made up of thousands of tiny separate eyes. A butterfly sees in all directions and detects movements very well. It can see things close up, but distant objects look blurry. A butterfly sees **ultraviolet** light waves that we can't see. This may help long-distance butterfly travelers, such as monarchs, to find their way.

Flower Food

Butterflies need lots of liquid and may visit hundreds of flowers in a day.

Wings of Beauty

Scientists group butterflies and moths into a category called Lepidoptera (leh puh DOP tuh ruh). *Lepidos* is a Greek word meaning "scales." *Ptera* is a Greek word meaning "wings."

The prettiest parts of a butterfly are its two pairs of wings. The forewings, located closest to the head, are often larger than the hindwings. The tops and bottoms of the wings usually have different patterns and colors.

The wings of butterflies and moths are covered with millions of tiny scales. Scales give the wings their color. The powder on your fingers after you touch a butterfly's or moth's wings is actually thousands of these scales!

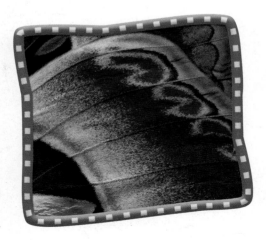

Colorful Scales

Earth tones, such as browns, reds, and yellows, on butterfly wings are created by coloring matter in the scales.

Some bold colors, like the blue on this morpho butterfly's wings, are not in the scales on the wings. The colors are created when light reflects off tiny ridges on the scales. When sunlight isn't shining on them, the morpho's wings look dull and colorless.

forewings

hindwings

Chapter 3

Feeding and Flying

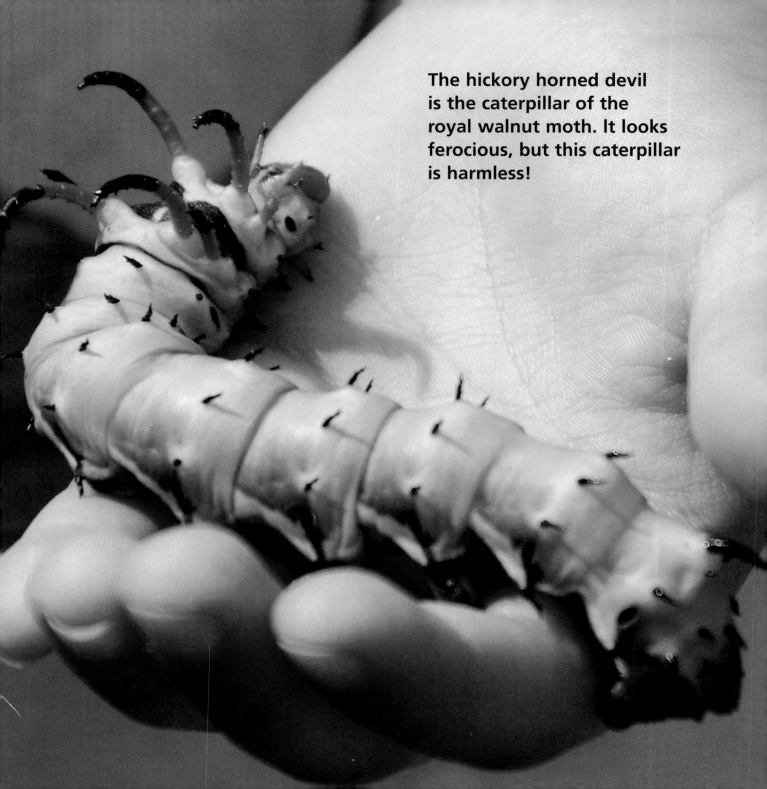

The hickory horned devil is the caterpillar of the royal walnut moth. It looks ferocious, but this caterpillar is harmless!

Eating Machines

Butterflies and moths develop in four stages: egg, caterpillar, **pupa**, and adult. The caterpillar is the feeding stage. All a caterpillar does is eat!

As the caterpillar eats, the cells in its body inflate like balloons. The caterpillar's body swells up so much that its skin splits. The caterpillar then wriggles free of its old skin. This process occurs about four or five times in a caterpillar's life.

Caterpillars have many **predators**, such as birds and other insects. Sometimes, though, there aren't enough predators to control caterpillar populations. Gypsy moth caterpillars, for example, sometimes chew up so many leaves in eastern oak forests that many oaks die.

Phony Feet

All caterpillars share a basic body design. The head has eyes, two tiny antennas, and chewing mouthparts. The body is made up of thirteen parts. The first three parts form the thorax, and each part has a pair of legs. The ten remaining parts form the abdomen. Five of those parts have a pair of false legs, called **prolegs**. The prolegs help the caterpillar move and grip twigs and leaves.

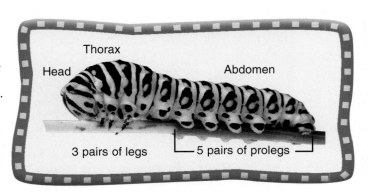

Thorax

Head

Abdomen

3 pairs of legs

5 pairs of prolegs

Flying Tales

If caterpillars are eating machines, butterflies are flying machines! Bad-tasting butterflies usually fly slower than butterflies that taste good. Predators don't chase them, so they don't have to fly fast.

The tiger swallowtail butterfly, however, tastes good and flies slowly. It has "tails" on its hindwings that look like antennas. When a hungry bird dives for what it thinks is the front end of the butterfly, it is left holding a bit of a wing tail! Meanwhile, the swallowtail has flown away to safety.

Stripes on the yellow forewings of these tiger swallowtails point to their swishing wing tails. If a hungry bird grabs the wing tails, the butterfly can still fly to safety.

Chapter 4
Surviving in the Wild

This caterpillar has curled its upper body to create a false head with two huge "eyes."

Caterpillar Tricks

Caterpillars feed out in the open, and they are slow moving. But caterpillars have ways of tricking hungry predators.

Some caterpillars have poisonous spines and prickly hairs that make swallowing them unpleasant. Others scrunch themselves into threatening positions when they are in danger. A few disguise themselves as bird droppings or other unappealing things!

Other caterpillars build structures to protect themselves from predators. Some moth caterpillars spin silk tents in which they rest when they are not feeding. Certain skipper butterfly caterpillars cover themselves with leaf tents.

Can You Find the Caterpillar?

The maple spanworm caterpillar is the color of tree bark. It can stretch out its body to look just like a twig!

Butterfly Disguises

Butterflies can escape from most predators by flying away. But flying won't work against birds and bats that can chase butterflies in the air. So some butterflies have colors and patterns that make them hard to see when they are resting on tree trunks or perched among leaves.

Warning Colors

Many butterflies stand out with bold colors that warn predators off. Some of these colorful butterflies are poisonous, so predators know to stay away. But several nonpoisonous butterflies also use warning colors to trick predators into looking elsewhere for a meal.

Eyes that Scare

When it opens its wings suddenly, a butterfly with eye spots can startle a predator long enough to escape.

Hanging off a leaf,
a resting butterfly looks
exactly like another
green leaf!

Dead Leaf?

Snout butterflies look like dead
leaves with stems. When they
fly in groups, they resemble dry
leaves blowing in the wind.

Chapter 5

Butterflies in the World

The peacock butterfly, a common butterfly of Asia and Europe, lives farther north than it once did because of climate warming.

All Kinds of Butterflies

There are about 15,000 different kinds of butterflies in the world. They live on every continent except Antarctica.

Tropical rainforests are home to the greatest variety of butterflies. The world's largest and rarest butterfly, the Queen Alexandra's birdwing, has a wingspan of up to 12 inches (30 cm)! It lives in the rainforests of Papua New Guinea, which is north of Australia.

Butterflies also live in the deserts, mountains, and Arctic **tundra**. The world's smallest butterfly, the Sinai baton blue, lives in the deserts of Egypt's Sinai Peninsula. It has a wingspan no wider than a thumbnail!

Big and Bad Tasting

The world's biggest butterflies, the birdwings of Southeast Asia, are bad tasting and poisonous. A predator only tries eating one once.

Perched on an orange slice, a painted lady butterfly sips juice with its proboscis.

proboscis

A Global Butterfly

Some kinds of butterflies live only in the wild where the plants they sip from grow. The painted lady butterfly isn't so picky. It eats from many different plants, so it can live in many different places—in the wild and in city and farm environments.

The painted lady can be found on all continents except Antarctica and Australia. It spends the winter in warm places where temperatures stay above freezing. In spring, painted ladies fly to places where they could not have survived in winter.

Colors that Change

A painted lady's wings are black, brown, orange, and white when opened. They are gray, tan, black, white, and pink when closed.

The Future of Butterflies

Many kinds of butterflies are **endangered**. Their numbers drop quickly when the wild plants that they eat and lay their eggs on become scarce. One of the best ways to help butterflies is to join an organization working to protect the natural **habitats** in which these beautiful and amazing insects live.

Fast Facts About Butterflies

	Monarch	Painted Lady
Scientific Name:	*Danaus plexippus*	*Vanessa cardui*
Order:	Lepidoptera	Lepidoptera
Family:	Danaidae	Nymphalidae
Size:	up to 3.9 inches (9.9 cm) wide	up to 2.9 inches (7.3 cm) wide
Life Span:	up to 6 months	about 2 weeks
Habitat:	fields, roadsides, seashore	fields, city lots, seashore

Some kinds of blue butterflies are endangered. One kind is extinct. It disappeared when its sand dune habitat was turned into a housing development.

Plant a Butterfly Garden

Even if you just have a window box, you can plant flowers that will lure butterflies. Butterflies like oxeye daisies, purple coneflowers, and marigolds. They like overripe fruit, too.

Glossary

abdomen — the rear part of an insect's body that takes care of breathing, digesting, and reproducing

antennas — a pair of organs on an insect's head for smelling and touching

caterpillar — the wormlike stage of a butterfly's development

chrysalis — a case that covers and protects a butterfly's pupa

endangered — a species of animal or plant in danger of extinction

forewings — the first pair of wings on a butterfly's thorax

gland — an organ that releases substances such as silk strands for attaching a chrysalis to a leaf

habitat — the natural environment where an animal or a plant lives

migrate — to go from one place to another at certain times of the year to find food or to mate and give birth

nectar — a sweet liquid made by flowers

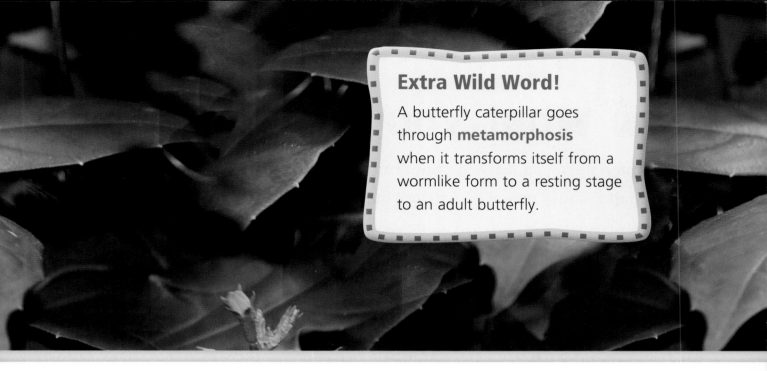

Extra Wild Word!
A butterfly caterpillar goes through **metamorphosis** when it transforms itself from a wormlike form to a resting stage to an adult butterfly.

predator — an animal that hunts and eats other animals to survive

proboscis — a butterfly's long, skinny mouthpart that works like a straw for sipping liquids

prolegs — stubby leg-like structures on the abdomens of caterpillars

pupa — the resting stage in a butterfly's life during which it changes from a caterpillar to an adult

species — a group of plants or animals that are the same in many ways

thorax — part of an insect's body located behind the head. Four wings and six legs are attached to it.

tundra — an area without trees in an Arctic region or on a high mountain with short plants and a frozen layer of soil underground

ultraviolet — light waves that cannot be seen by human beings

warning colors — markings and bright colors on an animal that warn off predators

Butterflies: Show What You Know

How much have you learned about butterflies? Grab a piece of paper and a pencil and write your answers down.

1. On what kind of plants do monarch butterflies lay their eggs?

2. What are the four stages of development in butterflies and moths?

3. About how many different kinds of butterflies are there in the world?

4. Where are a butterfly's sense organs located?

5. What is a butterfly's long mouthpart called?

6. How many pairs of legs does a butterfly have?

7. Which habitat is home to the greatest variety of butterflies?

8. How many times do monarch butterflies migrate in their lives?

9. What gives butterfly wings their color?

10. Which type of butterfly resembles a dead leaf with a stem?

1. Milkweed plants 2. Egg, caterpillar, pupa, and adult 3. About 15,000 4. On its head 5. Proboscis 6. Three 7. Tropical rainforest 8. Once 9. Scales 10. The Snout butterfly

For More Information

Books

Are You a Butterfly? Backyard Books (series). Allen, Judy and Humphries, Tudor (Kingfisher, 2003)

Eyewitness: Butterfly and Moth. Eyewitness Books (series). Whalley, Paul (DK Children, 2000)

From Egg to Butterfly. Start to Finish (series). Zemlicka, Shannon (Lerner Publications, 2002)

Web Sites

The Butterfly Website

http://butterflywebsite.com

Learn all kinds of facts about butterflies, including how to attract them and how to grow your own butterfly garden. You can also click on links to find more information about butterfly conservation groups.

The Children's Butterfly Site

http://www.bsi.montana.edu/web/kidsbutterfly

Find answers to frequently asked butterfly questions, coloring pages, and links to butterfly videos on this site.

Publisher's note to educators and parents: Our editors have carefully reviewed these web sites to ensure that they are suitable for children. Many web sites change frequently, however, and we cannot guarantee that a site's future contents will continue to meet our high standards of quality and educational value. Be advised that children should be closely supervised whenever they access the Internet.

Index